Vintage Anheuser-Busch®

Donna S. Baker

ORIGINAL BUDWEISER IN BOTTLES.

TRADE MARK.

An Unauthorized Collector's Guide

Schiffer Publishing Ltd

4880 Lower Valley Road, Atglen, PA 19310 USA

Budweiser
OUTSELLS ANY OTHER BEER IN AMERICA

It's the little things that make life friendly

Dedication

For Bales, a happy, hairy boy who is truly my "Bud."

Design by Blair Loughrey
Type set in *Benguiat BT/Korinna BT*

ISBN: 0-7643-0739-8
Printed in China
1 2 3 4

Published by Schiffer Publishing Ltd.
4880 Lower Valley Road
Atglen, PA 19310
Phone: (610) 593-1777; Fax: (610) 593-2002
E-mail: Schifferbk@aol.com
Please visit our web site catalog at
www.Schifferbooks.com
or write for a free catalog.
This book may be purchased from the publisher.
Please include $3.95 for shipping.

In Europe, Schiffer books are distributed by
Bushwood Books
6 Marksbury Rd.
Kew Gardens
Surrey TW9 4JF England
Phone: 44 (0)181 392-8585; Fax: 44 (0)181 392-9876
E-mail: Bushwd@aol.com

Please try your bookstore first.

We are interested in hearing from authors
with book ideas on related subjects.

Contents

Acknowledgments

I would like to extend my deepest appreciation to Peter C. Jordano, President and CEO of Pacific Beverage Company, whose willingness to share his company's wonderful collection of Anheuser-Busch memorabilia made this book a reality. I am grateful for Pete's generous cooperation and hospitality, as well as for the wealth of information he provided to assist with the project. JoAnn Cavaletto, of Jordano's Incorporated, was most helpful in making arrangements for me to photograph the collection and assisting with follow-up details afterwards. Everyone at Jordano's made us feel very welcome during our visit.

Harold Mann, antique advertising dealer and long-time member of the National Association of Breweriana Advertising (NABA), provided the values included in the book. I very much appreciate his assistance with this important facet of the project and am indebted to him for graciously sharing his experience and expertise.

My colleague Jennifer Lindbeck assisted with organizing the items to be photographed and recording information. Her common sense, mechanical sense, and sense of humor were all greatly appreciated. Thanks also to Tina Skinner, whose initial research and contacts got things going in the first place.

Introduction

What is it about early breweries, their history, and products that fascinates us so? Is it the tangle of buildings and smokestacks rising like mini-cities in the midst of industrious urban environments? The ability of those buildings and the workers inside to turn humble ingredients like barley, rice, hops, and yeast into a palate-pleasing, rousing beverage, the popularity of which has yet to wane? Perhaps it is the colorful stories surrounding many of the breweries' ambitious and enterprising leaders, or the industry's inexorable association with our country's Prohibition era, replete with its own stories of bootleggers and speakeasies. Surely, too, the appeal rests with an irresistible charm and nostalgia evoked by artifacts of the time: the posters and signs that hung on tavern walls, the serving trays and plates bedecked with multicolored pictures, the bottles and mugs embossed with brewery names, the advertising trinkets and assorted giveaways.

Of the many breweries that either flourished or floundered in the late 1800s and early 1900s, Anheuser-Busch represents the quintessential success story. Founded by the legendary Adolphus Busch, the company built its prosperity on quality products, innovative manufacturing techniques, and abundant, engaging advertising. Today it is the prevailing leader in the brewing industry, producing or distributing over thirty brands of domestic, imported, and non-alcoholic beverages,

managing twelve brewery locations, and operating multiple theme parks and other business ventures. Budweiser, the company's "flagship brew" introduced more than a century ago, is known, sold, and enjoyed worldwide. Adolphus would most certainly be proud.

This book chronicles the legacy of Anheuser-Busch through the many forms of advertising and related memorabilia produced by this historic company. The items presented are primarily from the company's earliest years through the mid-twentieth century, though you will find a few more contemporary pieces as well. Individual chapters highlight the wonderful assortment of company collectibles, from prints to pocket knives, mugs to matchsafes. While Budweiser advertising predominates, of course, items associated with the company's other products—many with interesting and noteworthy histories of their own—are included for your enjoyment as well.

Readers should note that the values listed in this book are intended to provide a general idea of what might be paid for the same or similar item in today's market. The values represent a guideline only and are not meant to "set" prices in any way. As with many other types of collectibles, prices may vary depending on such factors as age, condition, scarcity, geographic location, and the buyer's relative desire to own a particular item.

Chapter **1**

Perspectives:

The Early Years of Anheuser-Busch

Adolphus Busch, considered the founder of the company. Bronze bust with marble stand, made in Germany, c. 1913. 22" x 34". $3000 and up.

When Adolphus Busch arrived in the United States from Germany at the tender age of eighteen, it is probable that he already envisioned a successful future for himself. Born in 1839, Adolphus was the son of a successful merchant and businessman, was well-educated, and—obviously—confident enough to leave his native country and emigrate to the faraway city of St. Louis, Missouri.

Adolphus's arrival in 1857 coincided with a period of tremendous growth in the American brewing industry, so perhaps it is not surprising that this enterprising and energetic young man would gravitate to the beer business. The number of commercial breweries in the United States had grown from a little over a hundred in 1810 to more than twelve hundred in 1860, about the time that Adolphus Busch would have been looking for employment (Anderson 1973, 1). Initially, Adolphus worked as a brewery supplier, but his path took a fortuitous detour when he met and married a young woman named Lily Anheuser in 1861. Lily's father, Eberhard Anheuser, was the owner of a small, somewhat floundering St. Louis brewery he had acquired the year before as the Bavarian Brewery and renamed E. Anheuser & Co. At his father-in-law's urging, Adolphus began working as a salesman for the as-yet not very successful brewery, ultimately selling his former supply operation in 1869 and becoming a partner in E. Anheuser & Co.

From these historic beginnings, Adolphus soon became the guiding force behind the company, combining a keen marketing acumen and steadfast commitment to quality with innovative manufacturing and shipping techniques, building the company's production in the process from 8,000 barrels in 1865 to more than a million barrels by 1901. Among the technological advancements credited to Adolphus Busch in his early years with the company were the use of artificial refrigeration and pasteurization in the brewing process (both firsts in the industry), the development of refrigerated railcars able to transport beer safely over long distances, and the creation of railside ice houses designed to support the fleet of refrigerated railcars. Ten years after becoming a partner in E. Anheuser & Co., Adolphus saw his hard work rewarded with a change in the company's name: the brewery business first known as the Bavarian Brewery now officially became the Anheuser-Busch Brewing Association. One year later, in 1880, Adolphus Busch became president of the newly renamed company upon the death of Eberhard Anheuser.

The Anheuser-Busch brewery, as depicted in the centerfold of a 1914 booklet published by the company. 16" x 8.5". $50-75.

Metal sign, "Budweiser in Bottles," c. 1910. 7" x 17". $300-400.

BUDWEISER—
THE PRIDE OF ANHEUSER-BUSCH

Throughout its history, Anheuser-Busch has produced and sold more than fifty brands of beer and more than twenty types of non-alcoholic beverages, yet the company's proverbial fame and fortune has always been integrally tied to its "flagship brew," the world renowned Budweiser. Budweiser was born out of Adolphus Busch's desire to create and market a new beer, one that would appeal to a wide variety of tastes and have the potential to become a truly national brand. To that end, he studied European brewing techniques and, together with a St. Louis friend named Carl Conrad, developed a beer lighter in color and body than the prevailing brands of the time. He dubbed the new beer "Budweiser," a name he is reported to have liked for its prospective appeal to Americans as well as to German immigrants.

Embossed cardboard sign, "Anheuser-Busch Budweiser," c. 1917. 6" x 11". $100-150.

Budweiser Lager Beer was introduced to the public in 1876. For the first seven years of its production, Budweiser was brewed by E. Anheuser Co.'s Brewing Association (the name adopted by E. Anheuser & Co. upon its incorporation in 1875) but bottled and distributed by Carl Conrad. Conrad also first registered the Budweiser trademark in 1878. In 1883, however, Conrad's financial difficulties led him to sell his interest in Budweiser to Adolphus Busch. Although Busch did not actually acquire rights to the Budweiser name and trademark until 1991, from 1883 forward the Anheuser-Busch Brewing Association took over all facets of brewing, bottling, and distributing the soon-to-be legendary brand.

CURES AND CONNOISSEURS

In 1895, Anheuser-Busch began selling a malt-based health tonic known as Malt-Nutrine. This product, which remained on the market until 1942, was primarily intended for people of ill health who needed to build up their energy or fitness. Recommended for both adults and children, Malt-Nutrine was touted in advertisements as "nourishing, invigorating, appetizing, and strengthening," an "invaluable" aid for invalids, convalescents, and nursing mothers. Physicians were an important link in the marketing of Malt-Nutrine, as they could recommend or prescribe it for their patients. Anheuser-Busch distributed a series of tin advertising signs with distinctly medical themes to local physicians, hoping the signs would be hung in the physicians' offices or reception areas as a visual endorsement of the product.

Above: "C. Conrad & Co. Original Budweiser" embossed bottle. Carl Conrad, a friend and business associate of Adolphus Busch, was the original bottler and distributor of Budweiser beer. $35-50.

Left: Oval tin sign for Malt-Nutrine. 11" x 14". $500-750.

Fold out die-cut trade card for Malt-Nutrine, advertising the many professed benefits of this health tonic made by Anheuser-Busch. 9" x 16". $200-250.

Left: Malt-Nutrine tin sign, "A Hurry Call," c. 1915. This sign, depicting the urgent delivery of Anheuser-Busch's health tonic, was the kind distributed to physicians' offices as a reminder for them to recommend Malt-Nutrine to their patients. 12.75" x 7.75". $100-150.

Below: A second Malt-Nutrine tin sign, this one sometimes known as "Dr. Stork." However, as the note on the reverse side indicates, this picture was actually untitled when first distributed. 12.75" x 7.75". $100-150.

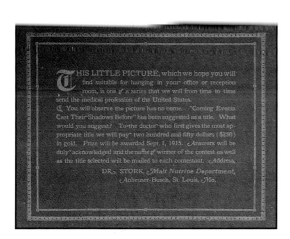

With Budweiser, Anheuser-Busch had intentionally created a beer for widespread sale and consumption; with Michelob—introduced twenty years later in 1896—the company set out to reach a more specialized market. An aristocratic product, Michelob was intended as a "draught beer for connoisseurs" and, true to that end, was not sold in bottles until 1961. Today it remains the superpremium beer among the contemporary family of Anheuser-Busch products.

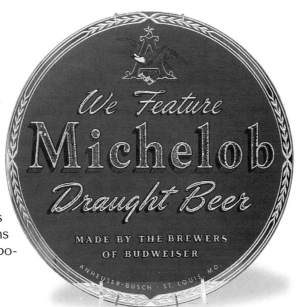

Reverse painted glass sign, "We Feature Michelob Draught Beer," gold leaf applied from the back, c. 1930. 10.75" dia. $150-200.

PROHIBITION YEARS

Adolphus Busch died in 1913, after spearheading the rise of a company that today is the largest producer of beer in the world. His son, August A. Busch Sr., succeeded him as president of the company. August Sr. already had considerable involvement and experience with Anheuser-Busch; he had been named general manager and vice president in 1909 and much of the brewery operations had fallen to him in the latter years of his father's life. Nonetheless, August Sr. was soon faced with a major business crisis of a nature his father never had to contend with: the imminent cessation of all beer and other alcohol production as a result of the 18th Amendment legislating National Prohibition in the United States.

The 18th Amendment was passed by Congress in December of 1917, however Prohibition did not actually take effect until midnight of January 16, 1920. On that date, the manufacture, sale, or transportation of alcoholic beverages became illegal in the United States and remained so for the next thirteen years. The effect of Prohibition on breweries was obviously a chilling one; for many, it led to their decline and ultimate demise. For August Busch Sr., Prohibition was an unwelcome, but not undefeatable adversary. Anheuser-Busch's *Annual Report, 1997* describes the challenges faced by August Sr. as he assumed responsibility for the company founded by his father:

> Instead of contributing to the company's growth—the role for which he'd been carefully groomed—he found himself struggling to simply survive. It is a tribute to his ability and determination that through these dark days, he was able to keep the company solvent and workers employed. (p. 22)

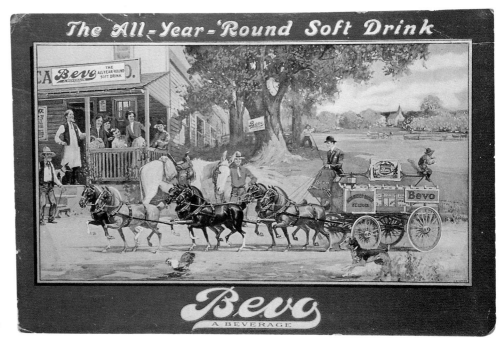

Cardboard sign for Bevo, horse and wagon team delivering cases of the "all-year-'round soft drink" to eagerly awaiting customers, c. 1920. 11" x 17". $175-225.

Bevo tin sign, cut in the shape of a bottle. 7.5" high. $400-500.

Left: Busch Extra Dry Ginger Ale bottle, c. 1920s. 9.75" high. $50-75.

Below: Embossed cardboard sign for Anheuser-Busch Ginger Ale. 11" x 6". $100-150.

August Sr. kept the family business alive during Prohibition by developing and selling a wide range of non-alcoholic products and by diversifying operations to include—among others—the construction of auto truck bodies, manufacture of refrigerated cabinets, rental of warehouse facilities, and sale of heat and power to other companies. In addition, he decided in 1922 to forgo his own personal salary until the company was on more secure financial ground.

Many of the products manufactured by Anheuser-Busch during the Prohibition years are colorfully reflected in the signs, trays, bottles, and other items favored by collectors. The most prevalent of these advertise Bevo, a cereal-based beverage widely distributed between 1916 and 1929. Note that 1916 predates the arrival of Prohibition: August Sr. was well aware of growing anti-alcohol sentiment and foresighted enough to develop Bevo in anticipation of the coming ban on beer. Other non-alcoholic beverages developed and sold by Anheuser-Busch during Prohibition include Buschtee, Kaffo, Ginger Ale, Extra Dry Ginger Ale, Old Devon Root Beer, and Grape Bouquet. As might be expected, some of these were more successful than others; Buschtee and Kaffo, for example, were tea and coffee flavored soft drinks that were—based on their lifespan of less than a year—apparently not very popular. In contrast, Extra Dry Ginger Ale and Old Devon Root Beer were both introduced the year after Buschtee and Kaffo (1921) but remained in production until 1942, well past the Prohibition era.

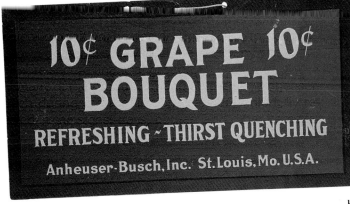

Embossed cardboard sign for "refreshing, thirst quenching" Grape Bouquet, a Prohibition era non-alcoholic beverage. 11" x 6". $100-150.

The sale of brewing process by-products was another avenue used by Anheuser-Busch to remain solvent during the years when brewing and selling beer was not an option. Barley malt syrup and baker's yeast were among the most successful of these. Barley malt syrup, a product used in the commercial baking industry, was manufactured from 1921 to 1954, while Anheuser-Busch yeast—the most enduring of the Prohibition era products—was in continual production from 1927 through the 1990s.

In 1919, the company name changed again, this time to Anheuser-Busch, Incorporated. This change is a useful tool for estimating the age of many Anheuser-Busch collectibles, as those marked Anheuser-Busch Brewing Association obviously date from 1879 to 1919 while those marked Anheuser-Busch, Inc. date from 1919 on.

Bulk canister for Barley Malt
Syrup, c. 1930. 14" high.
$200-250.

Paper labeled tin can, Budweiser
Barley Malt Syrup, c. 1930. 5" high.
$50-75.

Rectangular tin can to hold "Busch Healthrise"
yeast cakes. 4.5" x 3.5", 2" deep. $125-150.

CONTINUED GROWTH

August A. Busch Sr. lived to see the repeal of Prohibition in 1933, but died the following year, after twenty-one years of Anheuser-Busch leadership. Taking his place at the helm was his son, Adolphus Busch III, who steered the recovering company through the remaining Depression years and World War II. It was not easy to recover the energy and financial solvency of the company's earlier times, but production moved steadily forward and the two million barrel mark was achieved in 1938. One of the most significant changes during this period was the introduction of Budweiser beer in cans, a new form of packaging first begun in 1936. The beer-drinking public had to be convinced that Bud from a can was every bit as tasty as Bud from a bottle.

Adolphus III died in 1946 and his brother, August A. Busch Jr., succeeded him as president. Under August Jr.'s leadership, the company expanded dramatically, building additional breweries, adding Busch Beer to its line-up of brands, and opening Busch Gardens theme parks in Florida and Virginia. By 1975, when August Busch III became president—the fifth Busch to serve in that capacity—production had reached more than thirty-five million barrels. As of this writing, August Busch III remains the company's president.

Four Generations of Busch Family Leadership

Name	Relationship(s)	Birth/Death	Company Leadership
Adolphus Busch	—	1839-1913	1869-1913
August A. Busch Sr.	son of Adolphus	1865-1934	1913-1934
Adolphus Busch III	son of August Sr.; grandson of Adolphus	1891-1946	1934-1946
August A. Busch Jr.	son of August Sr.; brother of Adolphus III; grandson of Adolphus	1899-1989	1946-1975
August A. Busch III	son of August Jr.; great-grandson of Adolphus	1937-	1975-present

THE A & EAGLE TRADEMARK

In the earliest version of Anheuser-Busch's A & Eagle trademark, the eagle's wings were folded back into the A.

The use of trademarks was relatively unknown in the United States until the latter half of the nineteenth century. In 1866, when William and Andrew Smith began selling their Smith Brothers Cough Drops, however, they found it necessary to add a unique trademark to their packages to avoid confusion with similar looking products sold by their competitors. The United States Patent Office registered the first legal trademark, an eagle representing a New York paint company, in 1870 (Margolin, 32).

The second version of the trademark, used around the turn of the century, brought the eagle's wings outside the A and added radiating lines around the star at the very top.

This 1930s version of the A & Eagle appears similar to the one above, but the eagle's wings and beak are actually positioned quite differently. The Union Shield under the eagle's feet was replaced in 1939 with a horizontal striped shield.

Anheuser-Busch began use of its distinctive trademark, also based on an eagle design, only two years later in 1872. The "A & Eagle" was registered with the patent office in 1877 and has been used continuously since then as the official logo for Anheuser-Busch. The artist or creator of the trademark is not known. In fact, according to Anheuser-Busch's 1997 *Fact Book,* the origins of the A & Eagle remain an intriguing mystery:

> No record remains of the symbol's original designer or its exact meaning. The "A" stood for Eberhard Anheuser, but a question remains about the eagle. Some have said that it represents the unlimited vision of Adolphus Busch; others, that it was included as a mark of respect for America, the adopted country of the brewery's founder. Whatever the original meaning, the A & Eagle has come to symbolize the company's century-old heritage of pride and quality. (p. 40)

Although the basic elements of the A & Eagle have remained constant, various design changes have taken place throughout the years. As with the company's name changes, these variations in trademark design can help collectors in estimating the date of Anheuser-Busch items from the past.

Chapter 2

The Art of Advertising

A customer can't buy a product if he or she doesn't know it exists. To stay in business, a seller of goods or services must obviously make prospective customers aware that a particular item is for sale, and, furthermore, why *his* item is preferable to the similar one being sold down the street. Advertising, of course, is the process through which that information is communicated. As a culture, we are often fascinated by the many incarnations of advertising—the visual, aural, and written messages, the multitude of media used (today encompassing those blinking boxes popping up more and more on world wide web sites), the divergent themes ranging from comic to dramatic to sensual. Advertising from the past has a particular appeal, drawing us back to days we remember or have heard about, nudging sentimental or nostalgic memories to the forefront of our minds. William Ketchum notes that antique forms of advertising, or "advertiques," allow us to feel connected to the past in a way that many other items do not:

> One possible reason for the great popularity of these so-called advertiques is the fact that advertising is still a vital part of our society. With many other kinds of antiques, both the object and the function that it once performed are now obsolete. But the techniques employed in advertising have changed little since the nineteenth century, and posters, free samples, and mass advertising remain as much in use today as they were one hundred years ago. (Ketchum 1979, 152).

A distinction can be made between items created and used solely for advertising purposes (post-ers, signs, or trade cards, for instance) and those used for other, more utilitarian purposes that are simultaneously employed in an advertising capacity (think of a serving tray with an ad on the bottom, a corkscrew with the company name emblazoned across the top). Both have an allure and an appeal and both can be appreciated for their respective ability to attract the targeted consumer; both kinds are also featured within the pages of this book.

Among the myriad types of merchants and industries, breweries have traditionally used advertising extensively (and effectively) to promote their products; indeed, our country's beer brewers "probably produced more signs and trays than any other product group" (Cope, 13). Anheuser-Busch was certainly no exception—from the beginning, Adolphus Busch recognized the importance of courting the public, keeping his name prominently in customers' minds, and securing their ongoing loyalty to his brands of beer. Out of Adolphus's determination to build Anheuser-Busch into an industry leader (a determination passed on to his sons, grandsons, and great-grandson) has come a multitude of highly prized promotional items illustrating the two kinds of art found in brewery advertising: the "art" of achieving brand name allegiance and the "art" created by the beautiful and elegant subject matter of so many pieces.

Although the diversity of the company's advertising is one of its attractions, there are several prominent themes that characterize much of Anheuser-Busch's early advertising. Three in particular are beautiful women, western motifs, and the majestic Budweiser Clydesdales.

The Budweiser Girls

Attracting attention with the image of a comely woman has been a staple of advertising for many years; feminist issues aside, it remains just as popular today. For breweries, the combination of a beautiful woman and beer has been a favorite motif since the beginning of advertising (Haydock 1997, 115) From the late 1800s to the early 1900s, Anheuser-Busch took this concept one step further, creating a series of "Budweiser Girls" in a variety of styles and poses. Hung on the walls of local taverns, the Budweiser girls smiled down at customers, winsomely inviting them to enjoy a glass of this illustrious and popular brew.

Budweiser Girl in pink and yellow, upswept hair, one shoe demurely peeking from beneath her dress, c. 1904. She wears a pendant with the A & Eagle logo around her neck and holds a bottle of Budweiser. 19.5" x 35.5". $2000-3000.

Above: Dressed in native costume and holding a large glass of foaming beer, the "German Budweiser Girl," is featured on this early cardboard sign, c. 1890. Notice the A & Eagle logo incorporated into the first letter of the company's name at the bottom. Rare. 25" x 32". $3500 and up.

Left: The "Red Dress Budweiser Girl" is one of the images most widely associated with Anheuser-Busch. This lithographed sign shows her wearing a long-sleeved, high collar red dress, holding a bottle of Budweiser in her left hand and a pink rose in her right, c. 1907. 21" x 35". $1000-1200.

A variation of the "Red Dress Budweiser Girl" shows the same woman in the same pose, but wearing short sleeves instead of long. Lithographed sign, c. 1907. 21" x 35". $1200-1500.

BUDWEISER GIRL

Here is the "Fancy Dress Budweiser Girl," c. 1913. Last of the Budweiser Girls to grace an Anheuser-Busch sign, she wore a long elegant dress with a flounce at the bottom and a matching hat. Holding her dress up, she reveals black-stockinged legs and black high heels. 20" x 30". $2000-3000.

"Custer's Last Fight"

The infamous Battle of the Little Bighorn, commonly known as the "Last Stand" of George Armstrong Custer, took place in 1876, the same year that Anheuser-Busch first introduced Budweiser beer. A former Civil War officer, Custer became a lieutenant colonel of the Seventh Regiment U.S. Cavalry after the war and was involved in the nineteenth-century campaigns against Native Americans. His well-known last battle was fought in what is now southeastern Montana, where the U.S. Army was trying to protect gold prospectors from hostile Sioux and Cheyenne Indians. The troops under Custer's command were the advance scout portion of a three-way strategy designed to overpower the Indians. On June 25, 1876, Custer and his men attacked an encampment of Sioux they had discovered the day before, but woefully underestimated the number of Sioux warriors they ultimately faced. By the time the battle ended, Custer and his entire command of more than 250 men had been killed.

"Custer's Last Fight," lithographed print by F. Otto Becker for the Milwaukee Lithographic Company, in original advertising frame, c. 1904. 38" x 48". $1200-1400.

This last battle of Custer and his men became a popular subject for artists all over the country, immortalizing the troops' lamentable fate. One such artist was Cassilly Adams, whose large and dramatic image of the battle eventually hung in a St. Louis tavern that was purchased in 1888, painting and all, by Adolphus Busch.

As an astute businessman and constant purveyor of new advertising techniques, Adolphus soon recognized the potential of Adams's painting and its subject matter as a way to promote the Anheuser-Busch name. Although the original painting was later given to the Seventh Regiment, Adolphus commissioned a lithographic print of Custer's Last Fight to be done by another artist of the day, F. Otto Becker. Becker, who worked for the Milwaukee Lithographic Company, completed his version of the battle scene in 1896. Printed with the company's name at the bottom—"Anheuser-Busch Brewing Association"—and displayed in taverns across the country, the lithograph was an exceptionally successful advertising tool, demonstrating once again Adolphus's keen intuition for ways to promote his company.

A later version of "Custer's Last Fight," c. 1930. 35" x 46". $300-500.

The Budweiser Clydesdales

Double postcard depicting "one of the magnificent eight-horse hitches of the international champion Clydesdales," c. 1920s. 13.75" x 6". $20-30.

An advertising image that has endured for generations, the team of nattily attired Budweiser Clydesdales has been a perennial favorite of Anheuser-Busch fanciers from all over. Powerful yet gentle, the Clydesdale breed of horses is descended from Scottish draft horses originally used in a valley along the River Clyde, southeast of Glasgow. First recognized as an official breed in 1878, these stalwart giants generally stand at least six feet high when fully grown and can weigh more than two thousand pounds. They have a long and graceful stride, visually augmented by the white feathering on their feet and ankles.

Clydesdales were first brought to the United States in the mid-nineteenth century, where their size and strength made them a popular choice for work that involved hauling or pulling equipment. The Clydesdales' potential for more courtly labor was evident from the beginning, however, as Alix Coleman and Steven Price relate in *All the King's Horses*:

> Like other heavy horses, Clydesdales became an integral part of the American scene, pulling plows and other farm implements and drawing beer wagons and other vehicles. But Clydesdales were distinguished from other draft horses by their relatively finer features and eye-catching elevated leg action (especially enhanced by the white feathers). No matter how menial the task, the the Clydesdale gave the appearance of quiet authority, of being a true aristocrat among workhorses. (Coleman and Price 1983, 37)

Adolphus Busch and other members of the Busch family had long enjoyed horses and horse-related activities. Although images of Clydesdale horses appear on some early company advertising, the Clydesdales did not become the "living symbol" of Anheuser-Busch

and Budweiser until 1933, the year that Prohibition was repealed. To celebrate Prohibitions's end, August Busch Jr. purchased a team of Clydesdales, attached them to a Budweiser beer wagon, and presented them as a surprise gift to his father, August Busch Sr. Coleman and Price describe the events that followed this presentation, events that led the Clydesdales to continue as beloved representatives of the Anheuser-Busch company to the present day:

> August, Jr. had other plans for the Clydesdales. Realizing the tremendous potential of a horse-drawn beer wagon, he had the team sent by rail to New York City. After picking up two cases of beer that had been flown to New Jersey's Newark Airport, a six-horse hitch driven by [Billy] Wales trotted through the Holland Tunnel into Manhattan. When the team pulled up in front of the Empire State Building, the beer was presented to Al Smith, former governor of New York State, who had been instrumental in Prohibition's repeal. According to a newspaper account, more than five thousand people (a considerable crowd for a workday) rushed to see the presentation. (Coleman and Price 1983, 57-60)

Pocket knife decorated with the Anheuser-Busch Clydesdales. 3.5" long. $150-200.

Above: Plastic Budweiser advertising sign with Clydesdales. The red "bow tie" symbol for Budweiser was introduced by Anheuser-Busch in 1956. $75-125.

Right: Light up Budweiser sign with Clydesdale horse at rest. 19" x 14". $100-150.

Below: Large bubble lamp with Budweiser parade unit, featuring Clydesdales, beer wagon, and accompanying Dalmatians. The Dalmatians were added as mascots for the Clydesdales in 1950. 24" dia. $750-1000.

Crowds still turn out today for the Budweiser Clydesdales, long after that momentous occasion in 1933. Depictions of the majestic Clydesdale team became (and remain) a popular form of advertising for Anheuser-Busch, one that people everywhere instantly associate with Budweiser. At present, Anheuser-Busch operates a large Clydesdale breeding program and maintains three traveling hitches that tour the country, entertaining beer-lovers and their families with each impressive performance.

Chapter 3

Framed Prints and Posters

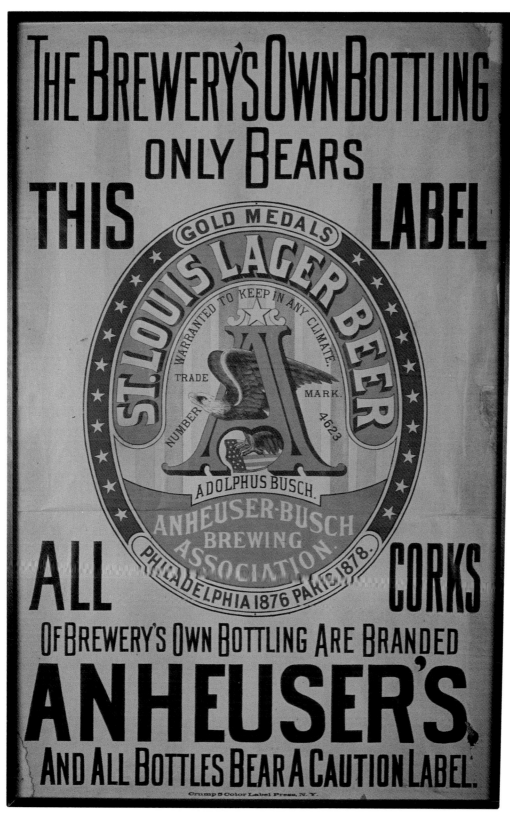

Very early lithographed advertising print for St. Louis Lager Beer, c. 1870. St. Louis Lager was brewed by Anheuser-Busch from the 1860s to the early 1900s and was considered the company's "flagship" brand prior to the development of Budweiser. 27.5" x 47.5". $1200-1500.

Paper sign, Anheuser-Busch Bock Beer, c. 1880. Bock is a type of beer, not a specific brand name. Many breweries produced bock beer; at Anheuser-Busch, it was brewed between 1879 and the mid-1950s. Notice how the eagle in the Anheuser-Busch logo on this sign has been replaced with a goat jumping through the red A. Goats were commonly associated with bock beer, possibly because of the beer's origin in the German town of Einbeck. The name "Einbeck" may have been distorted into the words "ein bock," meaning "a goat" in German. Very rare. 25" x 35". $2500-3500.

Anheuser-Busch Bock Beer poster, c. 1890. Now the eagle in the logo has reappeared, but seems to be sharing a glass of beer with the goat! 29" x 38". $2000-2500.

Lithographed paper sign, woman in long flowing gown, A & Eagle at top and bottom, c. 1890. Very rare. 16.5" x 33.5". $3500 and up.

Advertising card in early frame, "With compliments of Anheuser-Busch Brewing Association," c. 1893. 10" x 12", including frame. $100-125.

Gold framed paper sign, three young woman enjoying glasses of beer, "'Exquisite' Bottled Beer." 24" x 33". $3500 and up.

Richly colored lithograph print of woman holding beer glass in her
right hand and shield with A & Eagle in her left, goat in bottom left
corner. "Anheuser-Busch Beer, America's Favorite." 25" x 31".
$3500 and up.

Paper lithographed sign in original Anheuser-Busch
frame, eagle from trademark lighting on young
woman's hand. 28" x 36", including frame.
$2500-3500.

A reproduction of the earlier sign,
c. 1950. 13.5" x 18.5". $75-100.

Pair of lithographed indoor hanging signs, same image advertising different brands of beer, c. 1900. 23.5" x 33.5". $3000-3500 each.

Framed print, nude woman on craggy mountain top surveying the Anheuser-Busch brewery buildings. 39" x 31", including frame. $3500 and up.

Detail from the above print.

Gold framed print, "Anheuser-Busch Bock Beer," goat, dog, and glass of beer on tree stump. 18" x 21". $400-500.

A similar print, this one for "Budweiser Bock Beer." There is a slight variation in the glass and stump and no logo in the upper right corner. 16"x 20". $400-500.

Hop Picking for the Anheuser-Busch Brewing Ass'n, St. Louis, U. S. A.
AT SAAZ (BOHEMIA)

Indians Picking Hops for the Anheuser-Busch Brewing Ass'n, St. Louis, U. S. A.

Two lithographed advertising prints, hop picking
scenes, c. 1904. 17.5" x 13.5". $100-150 each

Above: Framed print, Clydesdales at rest with beer wagon. 28" x 12". $250-300.

Left: Framed Budweiser girl, cut from a larger sign, c. 1904. 11.5" x 13". $200-300, as is.

Decal on glass sign of the Red Dress Budweiser Girl, c. 1907. Rare. 13.5" x 17.5". $3000 and up.

Framed poster, same image as the Fancy Dress Budweiser Girl but here promoting Anheuser-Busch malt, c. 1913. $2000-3000.

Above: Framed print of elegantly dressed woman with hat, "Compliments of Anheuser-Busch." Very rare. 27" x 35". $3500 and up.

Left: Poster of young girl sitting on eagle's wings. $2500-3000.

Decal on wood, the "Modern Version of Ganymede," c. 1900. Ganymede was a figure from Greek mythology, a young Trojan prince who became cupbearer to the gods. He was carried off to Mount Olympus by the god Zeus, who appeared in the form of an eagle. Very rare. 20" x 30". $1000-1500 (this same image can be found on a tin sign, shown on page 49).

Framed advertisement, "The Triumphal
March of Bevo," c. 1910. 13" x 19". $25-50.

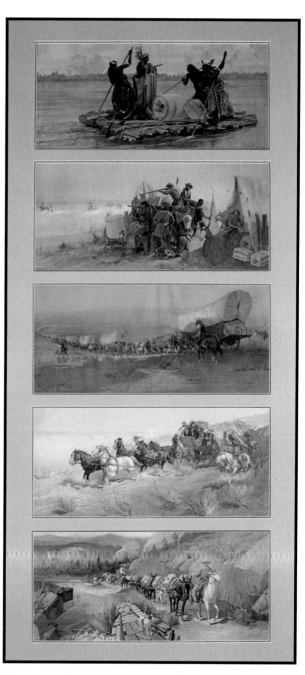

Framed set of western theme prints by St. Louis artist
Otto Berninghaus, c. 1914. Berninghaus was commissioned by August Busch, Sr. to paint a series of pictures
illustrating the westward expansion of America.
Anheuser-Busch later published a small booklet with
the same images in a reduced size. 24" x 47.5"
(individual prints: 16" x 7"). $1000-1200.

Opposite & above: Detail of the five western prints by Otto Berninghaus. $200-250 each.

Framed World War I advertising sign, "The Two Bismarcks," c. 1916. Note that the frame colors mirror those of the German flag. 17.5" x 22.5". $750-1000.

Chapter 4

Signs

Cardboard Signs

Above: Cardboard sign, "Tom, Dick, and Harry," in original advertising frame, c. 1904. 41.5" x 33". $1500 and up.

Right: Self framed cardboard sign, "Attack on the Overland Stage, 1880." This large sign illustrates well the western theme that was popular in early advertising. 41.5" x 28". $150-200.

Embossed cardboard sign, c. 1917. 6" x 11". $150-200.

Cardboard Budweiser sign, c. 1930s. 11.5" x 12". $125-150.

Cardboard sign announcing the arrival of Budweiser in cans, c. 1936. Perhaps the word "genuine" was included to assure consumers that although the packaging had changed, the beer itself was identical. $175-200.

Cardboard advertising sign
for draught beer. 11" x 6".
$150-175.

Cardboard sign for
Budweiser in bottles, c.
1930. 16.75" x 10.5".
$175-200.

Cardboard Budweiser sign advertising a
"new low price." 29" x 12". $75-100.

Above: Framed card for Busch Lager, "Makes All Food Taste Better." 13" x 22". $500-600.

Left: Framed cardboard sign for Busch Extra Dry Ginger Ale, c. 1930. Extra Dry Ginger Ale was produced from 1921 through 1942. 12" x 38". $250-300.

Cardboard advertising sign, maître d' advising waiters that "they'll all want Budweiser," c. 1935. 32" x 14". $200-250.

Framed sign for Budweiser malt, "The Best Money Can Buy."
Barley Malt Syrup, a brewing process by-product, was produced
by Anheuser-Busch from 1921 to 1954. 60" x 29". $200-250.

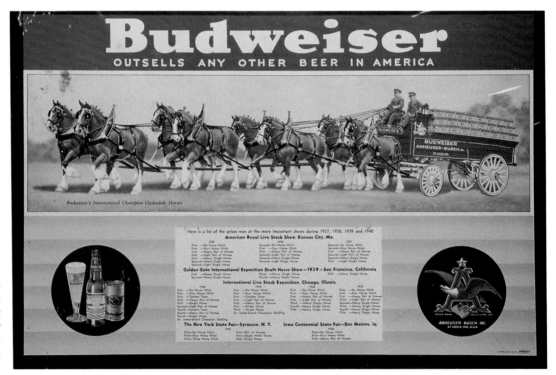

Cardboard sign
picturing the Budweiser
Clydesdales, c. 1940.
The center insert lists
the prizes won by the
Clydesdales at horse
shows held around the
country. 20" x 13.5".
$150-200.

Two cardboard advertising signs both inviting beer drinkers to "Make this Test: Drink Budweiser for five days. On the sixth day try to drink a sweet beer. You will want Budweiser's flavor thereafter." Sign with waiters: 20" x 28". Sign with woman: 10" x 17". $175-200 each.

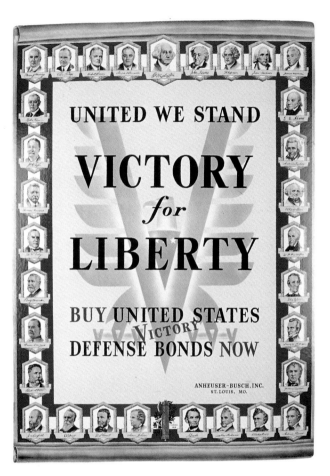

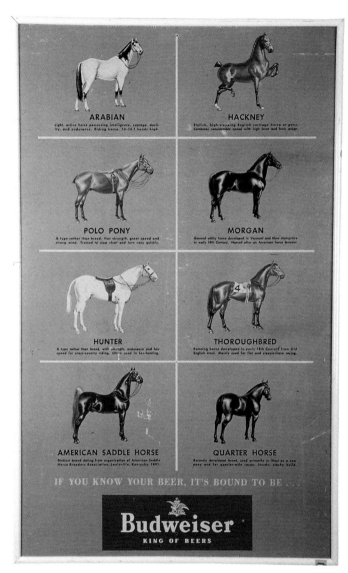

Above left: Cardboard sign promoting United States defense bonds, U.S. presidents around the perimeter. 17.5" x 24". $100-125.

Above right: Cardboard sign illustrating different types of horses, c. 1940. "If you know your beer, it's bound to be . . . Budweiser." 23" x 36". $100-125.

Right: Cardboard advertising sign for Budweiser with group of engaging Cocker Spaniel pups, "It's the little things that make life friendly." 14" x 15". $150-175.

Above: Embossed metal sign, c. 1904. Very rare. 28" x 32". $3500 and up.

Right: Detail from self framed tin sign, waiter serving elegantly dressed passengers in dining car, c. 1904. 22" x 28". $3000 and up.

Self framed tin sign, woman in pink holding
Budweiser bottle, c. 1904. Note the A &
Eagle pendant around her neck. 22" x 28".
$5000 and up.

Self framed tin sign, young woman in
garden with Budweiser bottle, c. 1900.
$3500 and up.

Opposite: Embossed metal sign,
"The Mirror of Truth," c. 1900.
25" x 38". $3500 and up.

Embossed metal sign, four little girls holding large tray with Budweiser bottle
and small trays with glasses, c. 1900. 18" x 26". Rare. $2000-3000.

Self framed tin sign, another image of the "Modern Version of Ganymede." 25.5" x 37.5". $3000 and up.

Self framed tin sign, "Malt-Nutrine, a Food Tonic," c. 1904. 20" x 16". $1200-1500.

Tall outdoor sign picturing early Anheuser-Busch Budweiser bottle, c. 1904. 12" x 37". $500-600.

Three oval tin plaques, c. 1904. 12" x 8". Top and middle: $750-1000. Bottom: $200-250, as is.

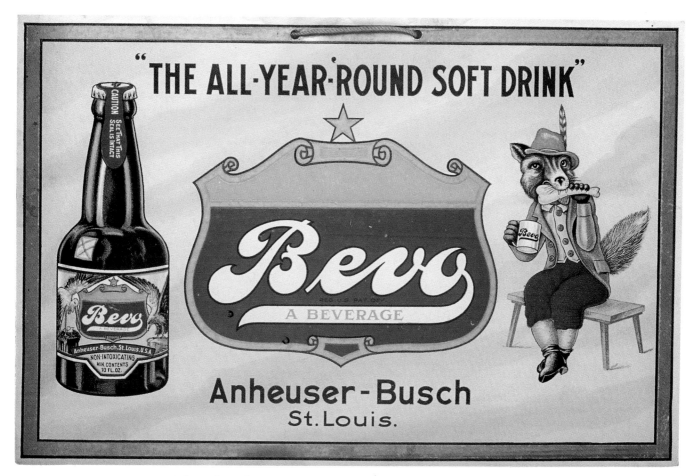

Embossed metal sign advertising Bevo, c. 1920. Bevo was a non-alcoholic beverage manufactured by Anheuser-Busch from 1916 through 1929. The Bevo fox, modeled after one from a Grimm's fairytale, appears on some of the signs and other advertising for this product. 12.5" x 8". $150-200.

Long metal sign for Bevo, "The All-Year-'Round Soft Drink," c. 1920. 28" x 7". $250-300.

Embossed metal Bevo sign. 27" x 13". $200-250.

Above: Tin Bevo sign. 9.5" x 6.25". $300-400.

Right: Another tin Bevo sign. 9" x 5.5". $125-175.

Framed tin sign, "Anheuser-Busch Lager Beer." 23" x 18", including frame. $3500 and up.

Hanging metal sign advertising draught beer, c. 1918. 10" dia. $300-400.

Tin sign for Extra Dry Ginger Ale, c. 1930. 9" x 13". $400-500.

Metal outdoor sign for Extra Dry Ginger Ale, "America's Finest," c. 1935. 21" x 11". $250-350.

Two-sided metal outdoor sign for "Budweiser, King of Bottled Beer," c. 1930. 18" x 13". $400-500.

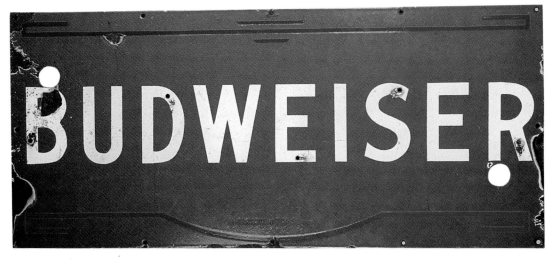

Metal outdoor sign for Budweiser, c. 1918. The two large holes on each end were for the mounting of neon light tubes. 36" x 15.5". $300-400.

Tin sign, "Anheuser-Busch, Original Budweiser." 13" x 6". $2000 and up.

Metal Faust beer sign. Faust was a brand of beer originally brewed by Anheuser-Busch especially for A. E. "Tony" Faust, owner of the St. Louis based Oyster House and Restaurant. Faust was sold nationally until 1942. 15" x 6". $250-300.

Faust "New Flavor" embossed metal sign, c. 1930s. The flavor may have changed, but the price remained the same! $350-400.

Lithographed tin sign with the Budweiser Clydesdales, c. 1930. 13" x 6.25". $250-350.

Tin indoor hanging sign, bottle of
Budweiser sitting on wooden case,
c. 1933. 7" x 17". $350-400.

Above: Framed tin
Budweiser sign. 16" x 41".
$2000 and up.

Left: Metal sign in Spanish
for Malt-Nutrine, c. 1930.
The message translates to:
"Nutritious Beverage for
People of All Ages." 11" x
23". $300-400.

Tin sign, "Budweiser Preferred Everywhere." 12" x 15". $150-200.

Metal outdoor sign proclaiming Budweiser "The Nation's Favorite Beverage," c. 1935. 21" x 11". $400-450.

Metal Budweiser sign with curved sides, "Makes Good Food Taste Better." 37" x 17". $200-250.

Tin sign, cut out in the shape of a label. 12" x 6". $800-1000.

Tin sign, Budweiser bottles on each end. 27" x 5". $200-250.

Above: Tin "Welcome" door push, smiling waiter uncapping bottle of Budweiser. Rare. 3.5" x 11". $300-400.

Left: Metal Budweiser sign, "King of Bottled Beer" slogan, c. 1930-1940. 9" x 15". $150-200.

Metal Budweiser sign with fancy gold lettering. 15" x 6". $125-150.

Tin door push originally used on grocery store screen door, c. 1940. 4.5" x 10". $200-250.

Metal hanging sign, "Budweiser Preferred Everywhere" slogan, c. 1940. 12" x 15". $150-200.

Glass Signs

Above: Elegant, reverse painted glass sign in ornate wooden frame, "Anheuser-Busch Bottled Beer." 25.5" x 28.5", including frame. $4000 and up.

Left: Reverse painted glass sign advertising Budweiser, gold leaf applied from the back, c. 1930. Reverse on glass signs are designed and painted on the back, where the texture accepts the paint more readily. The often brilliant colors are viewed through the front of the glass, which acts in a protective capacity for the paint. This technique was quite expensive, requiring much detailed handwork. 10.75" dia. $150-175.

Left: Curved glass corner sign, "Anheuser-Busch St. Louis Beer," large A & Eagle at top. This type of sign would have been mounted on the outside corner of a tavern. 15" x 26". $3000 and up.

Below: Reverse painted glass sign, gold leaf applied from the back, c. 1930. 12" x 4". $150-175.

Above: Glass sign for Michelob, "The Great American Beer in Bottles." 12" x 8". $175-200.

Right: Reverse painted glass sign, gold leaf applied from the back, c. 1930. 14" x 8.5". $175-200.

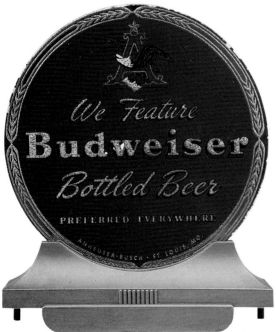

Above: Reverse painted glass sign on metal base, c. 1930. 10.75" dia. $200-250.

Right: The same glass sign enclosed within a round wooden frame. $200-250.

Above: Glass Budweiser sign on wooden base. Sign only: 13" x 11". $175-200.

Left: Budweiser mirror with reverse painted glass, c. 1900. 10" x 6". $1750-2000.

Below: Round mirrored sign, "Drink Budweiser Beer." 15" dia. $800-1000.

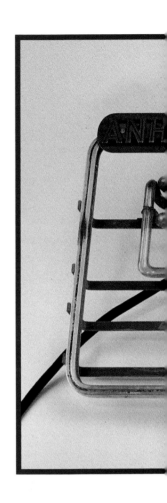

Round neon sign, c. 1930. "Budweiser" lights up in white
below the A & Eagle logo. 24" x 17". $250-300.

Rectangular neon sign, "Budweiser
on Tap." 27" x 12". $250-300.

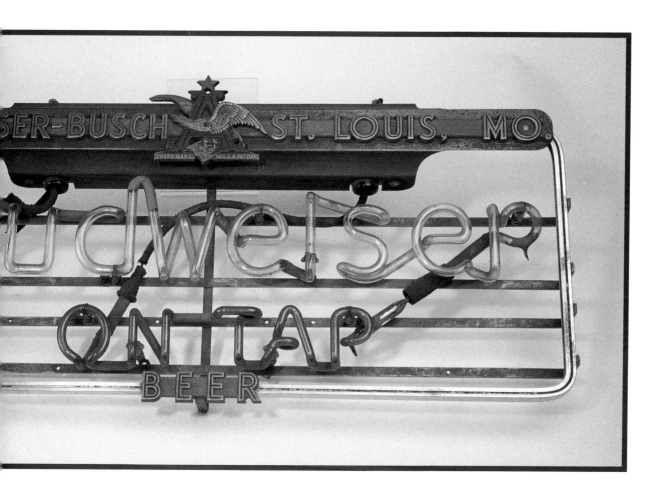

Above: "Budweiser" lights up in pink when the rectangular sign is plugged in.

Left: Round neon sign with scrolled wrought iron trim. 27" dia., including trim. $800-1200.

Chapter 5

Calendars

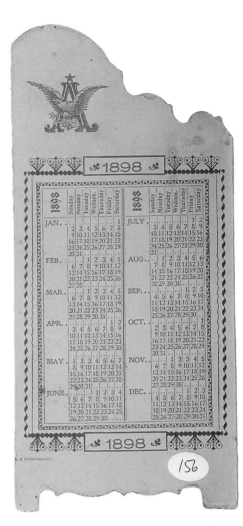

These early advertising cards for Malt-Nutrine feature an 1898 calendar on the reverse side as well as copy extolling the product's virtues. 4" x 8.5". $40-50 each.

Malt-Nutrine
round calendar,
1904. 12" dia.
$300-350.

Framed set of Anheuser-Busch calendar prints, lithe young women with flowing hair and gowns representing the four seasons, c. 1906. $2500 and up.

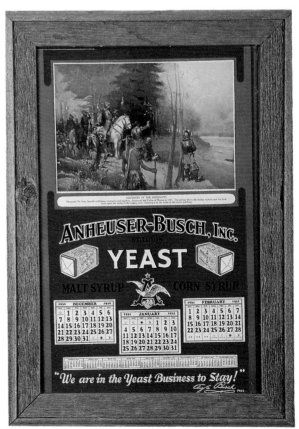

Anheuser-Busch calendar, "We are in the Yeast Business to Stay!" c. 1930. Also advertises malt syrup and corn syrup, two other products made by Anheuser-Busch. 18" x 25.5", including frame. $150-200.

Metal calendar with
cardboard date inserts,
c. 1940s. Distributed
by the Southern
Beverage Company,
Inc., Herrin, Illinois.
12" x 24". $150-200.

Chapter 6

Magazine Ads

Early magazine ad for
Malt-Nutrine,
Anheuser-Busch's
health tonic, c. 1920.
10" x 13.75". $15-25.

Above left: Framed magazine ad, c. 1934. 14" x 18", including frame. $15-25.

Above: Magazine ad hanger, c. 1935. 9" x 11". $15-25.

Left: Budweiser ad featuring horses and jockeys. 7" x 10". $25-35.

Magazine ads illustrating a variety of Budweiser slogans, c. 1940-1950. $15-25 each.

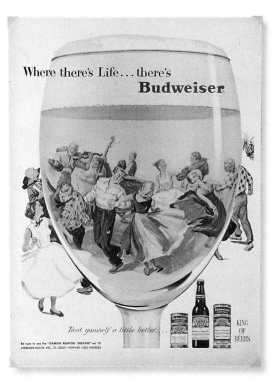

When Ice went on Wheels
Better Food went on Tables

In 1878, a new kind of train sped out of St. Louis. Its cars were loaded with barrels of Budweiser kept cold and fresh by ice-filled compartments. Thus, the brewing industry had its first refrigerator cars—and Budweiser had begun its journey toward 'round-the-world fame. Later, in the 80's, the refrigerator car made it possible for all parts of America to have fresh meat, fruits, vegetables and other good things of life.

Today, the delicious foods from far and near that make your table inviting need one thing to highlight their flavors. Golden, bubbling Budweiser brings out the fine flavor of food without losing its own distinctive taste. Every sip tells you why it is something more than beer— a tradition in hospitality.

Budweiser
TRADE MARK REG. U. S. PAT. OFF.

It lives with good taste everywhere

ANHEUSER-BUSCH . . . SAINT LOUIS

Chapter 7

Postcard Potpourri

$25-30.

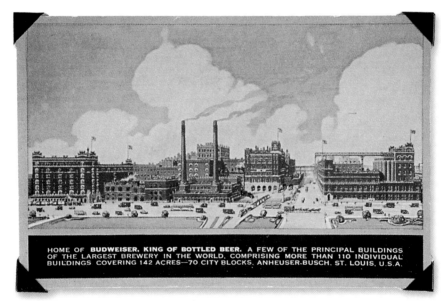

$25-30.

$20-25.

$10-15.

$5-10.

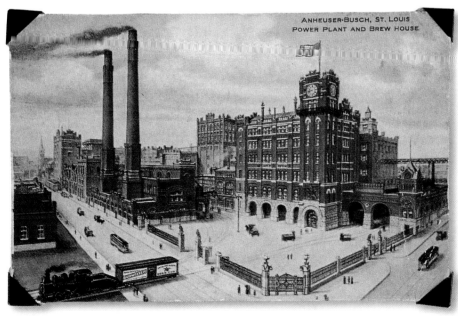

$25-30.

$5-10.

$15-25.

$15-25.

$25-30.

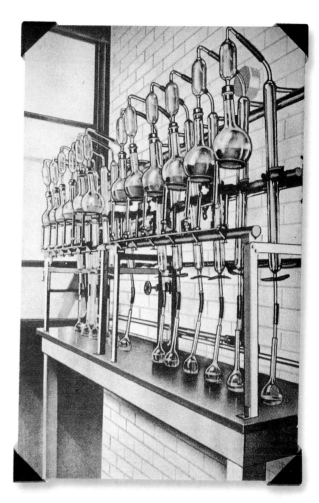

$25-30.

$25-30.

Greetings from Anheuser-Busch Brewing A[...]

BOTTLING DEPARTMENT, CAPACITY 800,000 BOTTLES DAILY.

Dearest Ma, Pa, & Lizzie Here we all drinking one [...] you — soon be with you Gust & Bert[...]

$25-35.

BUSCH PLACE, ST. LOUIS

$20-25.

Reception Room of ANHEUSER-BUSCH, ST. LOUIS — World's Largest Brewery

3A-H8[...]

$20-25.

"STERNEWIRTH"
ANHEUSER-BUSCH BREWING
PLANT, ST. LOUIS

$25-30.

ANHEUSER-BUSCH, ST. LOUIS
PRESIDENT'S PRIVATE OFFICE

$25-30.

Greetings from
Anheuser=Busch Brewing
Ass'n.

PRESIDENT'S PRIVATE OFFICE.

A CORNER IN THE DIRECTORS' ROOM.

$30-35.

$30-35.

$20-25.

$20-25.

1197 - Sunken Garden at Adolph Busch Residence, Pasadena, California.

$20-25.

Rose Hedge at Busch's Residence, Pasadena, Cal.

$20-25.

$50-60.

ONE OF THE MAGNIFICENT EIGHT-HORSE HITCHES OF CLYDESDALES USED BY THE LARGEST BREWERY IN THE WORLD — ANHEUSER-BUSCH, ST. LOUIS — BREWERS OF THE FAMOUS **BUDWEISER**, KING OF BOTTLED BEER.

$15-20.

$5-10.

ONE OF THE MAGNIFICENT SIX-HORSE HITCHES OF CLYDESDALES USED BY ANHEUSER BUSCH, ST. LOUIS, BREWERS OF THE WORLD FAMOUS BUDWEISER BEER

$15-20.

ONE OF THE MAGNIFICENT EIGHT-HORSE HITCHES OF INTERNATIONAL CHAMPION CLYDESDALES USED BY THE LARGEST BREWERY IN THE WORLD — ANHEUSER-BUSCH, INC., ST. LOUIS, MO. — BREWERS OF THE FAMOUS BUDWEISER, KING OF BOTTLED BEER.

$15-20.

$25-35.

$25-35.

$50-60.

Bevo Fox   Anheuser-Busch, Inc.

$10-15.

$50-60.

Opposite: $45-55 each

FAUST. PROLOGUE

You two, who stood by me so oft in times of distress and adversity come and drink a glass of Tony Faust Beer with me.

FAUST. Act I.

O glass of Tony Faust Beer bringing relief from earthly sorrow, why tremblest thou in my grasp.

STRADELLA

Let us hope that prayer granting,
All our efforts may be blessed;
That Budweiser Beer you deem enchanting
Find an echo in each breast.

MARTHA. Act III Sce. I.

PLUNKETT:
And that explaineth where er it reigneth is joy and mirth. At every hearth resounds a joyous song. Look at its goodly color here, where else can you find such brown, stout and healthy beer as Budweiser Beer.

$45-55.

$45-55.

Above & right: $5-10 each.

Chapter 8

Trays and Plates

Although their main purpose was a functional one, many of the early serving trays from the late 1800s to the early 1900s are miniature works of art, resplendent with detailed drawings and rich colors. As Will Anderson comments, "If breweriana in general is a colorful galaxy among twentieth-century collectibles, then trays are the brightest stars in that galaxy" (Anderson 1973, 27).

Decorated serving trays had their origins in the mid-1890s, around the time that the process of creating lithographed images on metal was perfected. Breweries recognized the potential of this standard tavern item as a valuable advertising commodity and began purchasing beautifully lithographed trays in large quantities; tray production between 1900 to around 1917 was particularly extensive. Most were produced by one of two advertising companies based in Coshocton, Ohio—Tuscarora Advertising and Standard Advertising—and came in round, oval, or rectangular shapes. The trays were most often adorned with pictures of the breweries themselves, the products they manufactured, beautiful women enjoying beer, fancy lettering, horses, and other animal figures. While many were unique to a particular brewery, some of the images (especially the beautiful women) were available on "stock trays," meaning that the same image could be found on trays from various companies. As might be expected, trays from the Prohibition years usually advertised the non-alcoholic products sold at that time.

Large tin serving tray ornately decorated with beer steins, known as the "Page Boy Tray," c. 1898. Very rare. 18.75" x 15.5". $3500 and up.

Above: Another early tray, this one depicting the brewery buildings of "America's Largest and Favorite Brewery," c. 1900. Sometimes known as the "Factory Scene Tray," this tray has four A & Eagle logos placed at the top, bottom, and sides of its border. 18.75" x 15.5". $1200-1500.

Right: Metal serving tray, known as the "A & Eagle Bull's Eye Tray," c. 1904. The concentric circles around the tray's perimeter lead the eye towards the A & Eagle logo in the center—the "bull's eye"—of the tray. 12" dia. $1000-1500.

Above: Metal serving tray, figure of woman holding large A & Eagle, winged cherubs surrounding her holding various Anheuser-Busch products, c. 1904. 16.5" x 13.5". This tray was also produced in a smaller size (12.5" x 10.5"). $1000-1200.

Left: The same woman and cherubs image appears on this tray, however it is printed on the outside—rather than the inside—of the tray, allowing it to also be used as a sign. 14" x 11.5". $800-1000.

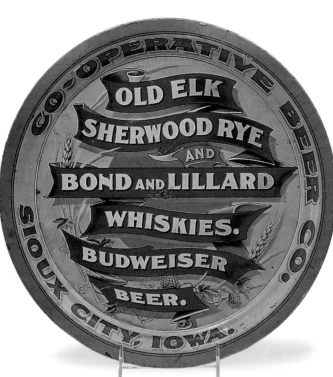

Above: Metal serving tray from a Sioux City, Iowa agency, showing Budweiser beer as one of its many brands, c. 1905. 13" dia. $500-750.

Right: Very early Anheuser-Busch oval metal tray. This was the first serving tray distributed by the company. 15" x 19". $5000 and up.

Metal serving tray advertising Bevo, the non-alcoholic beverage made during Prohibition years, c. 1920. 10.5" x 13.25". $125-150.

The same wagon and high-stepping horse team from above appear on this Bevo tray, c. 1930. This tray is seldom found with a red rim. 13.25" x 10.5". $125-150.

Bevo tip tray, c. 1920. 6.5" x 4.5". $200-225.

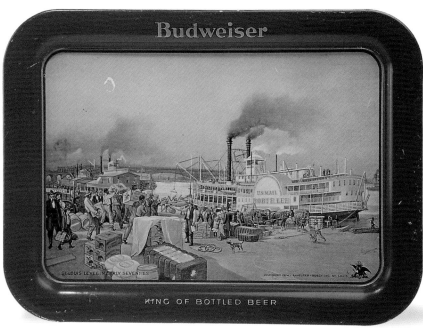

Above: Small metal tray, A & Eagle design. 5" dia. $100-150.

Right: Metal serving tray, "St. Louis Levee In Early Seventies," copyrighted 1914 but printed in 1930. 17.5" x 12.75". $150-200.

Above: Tin serving tray, "Ask Your Customers to Make the Budweiser Test," c. 1933. 13" dia. $75-100.

Right: Tin serving tray, another version of the "Budweiser Test," c. 1940. 13" dia. $50-60.

Metal serving tray, c. 1933. A shadow cast by the fireplace light on the tackle box resembles a fox, hence the pointing dog. 13.25" x 10.5". $100-125.

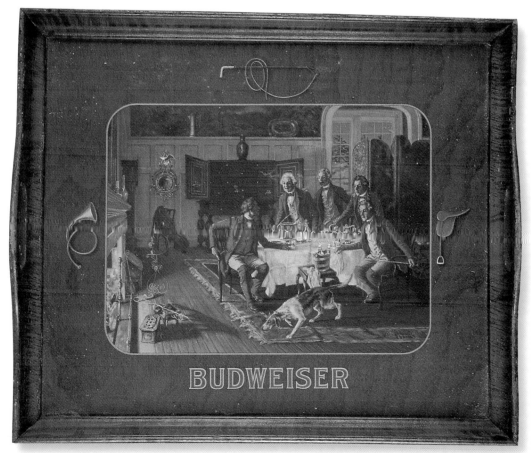

The same image appears on this slightly larger serving tray with handles. 13" x 16". $150-175.

Above: Metal serving tray. 13" dia. $50-60.

Right: Tin serving tray, c. 1940. 13" dia. $75-85.

Above: Tin serving tray, c. 1950. 13.25" dia. $35-45.

Right: Very heavy metal plate from 1876, possibly the cornerstone from a building. 8.5" dia. $300-400.

Above & right: Vienna art plates, Anheuser-Busch advertisement for Malt-Nutrine on reverse, c. 1904. 10" dia. $100-150 each.

Below: This plate and box are from the second edition of a series called "Vignettes of Early Anheuser-Busch," produced by Crown Bavaria Porcelain Works in Germany. This shows a reproduction of the Oscar Berninghaus painting, *St. Louis Levee.* 7.5" dia. $25-50.

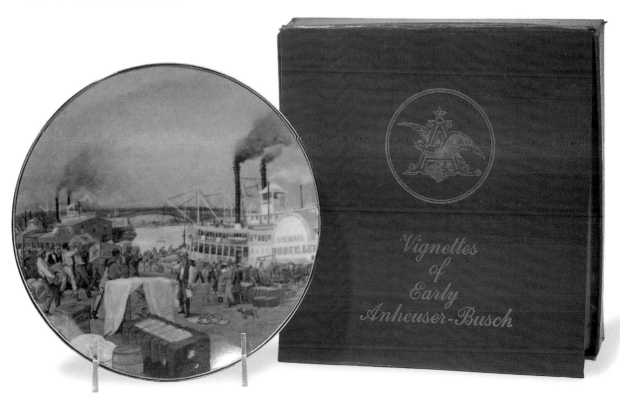

Plate from the fifth edition of the Vignettes series, depicting the 1914 *Say When* painting. 7.5" dia. $25-50.

The dining car scene from this plate was originally used on a tin sign from the early 1900s (see page 45). 7.5" dia. $25-50.

When Gentlemen Agree is the name of the image reproduced on this plate. 7.5" dia. $25-50.

Plate with Budweiser girl in short-sleeved red dress. 7.5" dia. $25-50.

Anheuser-Busch pewter plate. 9" dia. $50-75.

White china plate decorated with the Budweiser Clydesdales. 10" dia. $50-60.

Three piece china set, white with gold rim and the initials "AB." Dinner plate: 10.5" dia.; soup bowl: 9" dia.; bread and butter plate: 7.5" dia. $100-150.

Anheuser-Busch silver plates. 9.5" dia. $100-150 each.

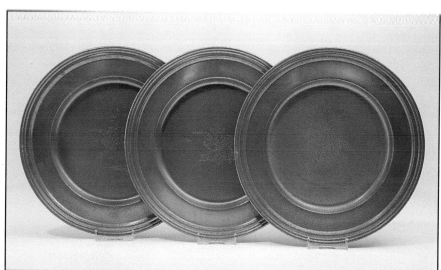

Chapter 9

Bottles and Cases

A look at some of these early bottles conjures up images of rakish, convivial gentlemen from the turn of the century, a lady or two on their arms, a bottle of Budweiser on the table in front of them. What tales these humble glass containers might relate! The manufacture of the bottles themselves, in addition to the beer they held inside, was a major undertaking for Anheuser-Busch. In an 1889 promotional booklet describing the "Origin and Unprecedented Growth" of the Anheuser-Busch Brewing Association, the company shared some statistics about their beer bottle production process:

> Of bottles, the Anheuser-Busch Brewing Association used during the past year nearly 27,000,000. These were all manufactured to order, and their cost was over $1,000,000. As they are made by hand, and as the labor is the chief cost of manufacture, it is clear that in the bottle industry a host of workmen are kept employed by this brewery alone. The Association operates a large bottle factory exclusively for its own supplies at Belleville, Ill.
>
> The barrels and boxes in which these bottles are packed for shipment all over the world numbered over 500,000 during the past year, and cost $200,000. These are made to order by outside establishments. (*A Simple Story* 1889, 11-12)

Anheuser-Busch embossed beer bottles, c. 1890-1910. Clear bottles: $40-50 each. Brown bottles: $25-35 each.

Above & left: Two early Budweiser bottles from "C. Conrad & Co." Budweiser was bottled and distributed by Carl Conrad from 1876 to1883. 9.5" high. $40-50 each.

Above: Dark blue beer bottle, c. 1890-1910. $150-175.

Left: Brown beer bottle c. 1910. 11.5" high. $45-55.

Anheuser-Busch embossed
beer bottles, c. 1890-1910.
$30-50 each.

Early labeled beer bottles, c. 1890-1910. From left: $25; $65; $85.

Above: Budweiser bottle with German label, c. 1900-1918. 12" high. $25-30.

Left: Two Budweiser beer bottles, one labeled in English, the other in German. 9.5" high. $25-30 each.

Malt-Nutrine and St. Louis Lager bottles, c. 1890-1910.
Heights range from 6.5" to 10". $30-85 each.

Another St. Louis Lager
bottle, c. 1890-1910.
The label attests to the
three gold medals from
World's Expositions
won by this early
Anheuser-Busch brand
of beer. 11.5" high.
$75-85.

Close-up of the back of the St. Louis Lager bottle.
This is the earliest version of the A & Eagle trademark, registered (as noted) in 1877.

Left: Anheuser-Busch Bock Beer bottle, c. 1890-1910. 9.5" high. $25-30.

Right: Budweiser bottle, "New Budweiser Brew." $15-20.

Additional Malt-Nutrine bottles, c. 1900-1918. $30-40 each.

Above: Busch Lager bottle, c. 1900-1918. 9" high. $60-75.

Left: Bevo bottle, c. 1910. 7.5" high. $25-35.

Above: Anheuser-Busch Root Beer bottle, c. 1910. 9.5" high. $50-60.

Left: Grape Bouquet bottle, c. 1910. This imitation grape syrup was produced by Anheuser-Busch from 1922 to 1928. 7.5" high. $45-55.

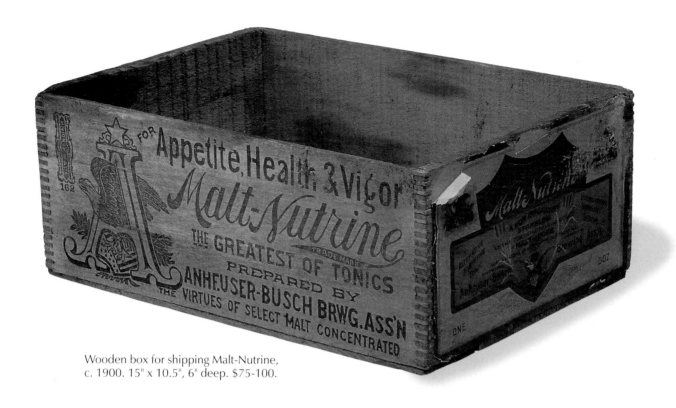

Wooden box for shipping Malt-Nutrine,
c. 1900. 15" x 10.5", 6" deep. $75-100.

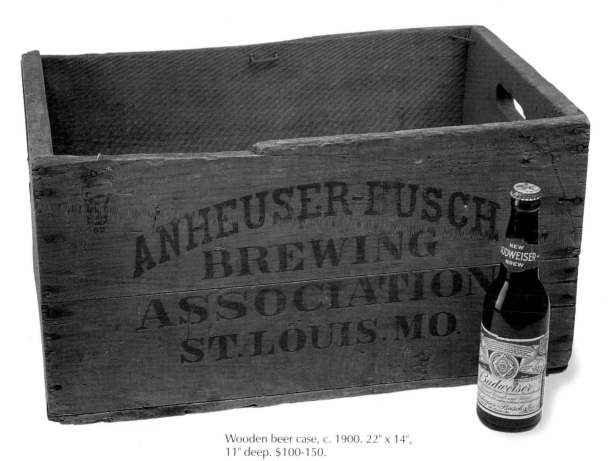

Wooden beer case, c. 1900. 22" x 14",
11" deep. $100-150.

Above: Wooden beer case with lid, c. 1910. 19.5" x 12.75", 11" deep. $75-100.

Right: The A & Eagle atop the lidded beer case.

Chapter 10

Cans

Cans are commonplace in the contemporary world of beer, but of course it wasn't always so. The first beer cans were developed in 1935 by the American Can Company and test marketed in Richmond, Virginia, by the C. Krueger Brewing Company of Newark, New Jersey. These pioneer cans consisted of three steel segments—a top, bottom, and body—and used a special lining on the inside trademarked "Keglined" by American Can. The purpose of the lining was to keep the beer from coming in contact with, and subsequently reacting to, the actual metal can. The top of the cans was flat and they were known by the descriptive, if not very imaginative, term "flat tops." Soon after the "flat top" cans were introduced, a short-lived variation can with a spout top was also given a tryout. Also known as a "crown top" or "cone top," the spout top cans were reminiscent of the shape of a bottle and could be opened more easily than the flat tops. However, they did not store as easily as flat tops and the latter soon bypassed them as the can of choice for most breweries.

The biggest challenge faced by Anheuser-Busch and other breweries in the '30s was convincing their customers that beer in cans was not only convenient, it was just as palatable as beer in bottles or on draught. The first five years of the can's history were especially prolific with respect to informing and educating the public:

> While the can had real advantages from the viewpoint of the brewer and the retailer, it had to be accepted by the beer-drinking public if it was to become more than a short-lived fad. As a result, in the period from 1935 to 1940 the can was promoted through the most expensive advertising campaign ever conducted for any kind of container. In addition, all early cans carried statements or even lengthy passages extolling the virtues of canned beer. (Anderson 1973, 57)

Flat top cans were discontinued in 1964; the year prior, Anheuser-Busch introduced its first all aluminum, two piece can. Tab tops, the can with the built-in opener, arrived in the 1960s. They were used first on steel cans and later on aluminum cans.

The earliest form of Budweiser cans, c. 1935-1950. These were designated "Eagle Claw" cans, also known as "winged." Several versions of "Eagle Claw" cans were manufactured, including a wartime version in olive drab instead of gold. 4.5" high. $50-75 each.

Gold Budweiser cans, designed to simulate the label on a bottle of Bud, c. 1950. A beer bottle was featured on the side of the can along with a reminder that Budweiser came in both bottles and cans. 4.5" high. $35-50 each.

Close-up of an "Eagle Claw" Budweiser can, c. 1935-50. $50-75.

Early cans like the one at left required a "church key" type opener and included opening instructions on the side of the can.

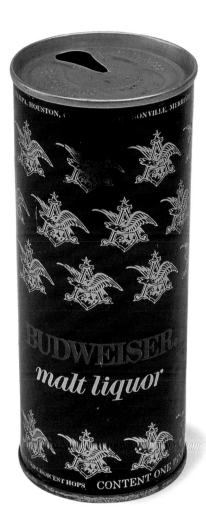

Another 1950s version of a Budweiser can. Note the three brewery sites at the very bottom of the label. From 1952 to 1977 Anheuser-Busch cans listed all the cities where Budweiser breweries were located. Current cans show only the location where the beer in that can was actually made. $35-50.

Budweiser Malt Liquor beer can, 16 oz. tab top, steel, c. 1971. 6.5" high. $75-100.

Chapter 11

Mugs, Steins, and Glasses

Early ceramic beer stein, Anheuser-Busch Brewing Association. Rare. 4" high. $2500-3500.

Ceramic mug with A & Eagle. The trademark design with the eagle's wings uplifted and rays emanating from the star atop the A is c. 1898. $750-1000.

Above: Ceramic mug, "Original Budweiser." 4" high. $500-750.

Left: Ceramic mug, Faust brand beer. 4" high. $750-1000.

Above: Ceramic Budweiser beer mug. 8" high. $25-40.

Above right: Anheuser-Busch occupational shaving mug, personalized for the owner. Very rare. 4" high. $2000-3000.

Right: Tall etched mug, A & Eagle. 8" high. $600-750.

Set of three Anheuser-Busch glass mugs. 5.25" high. $100-150 each.

Above: Glass Michelob beer stein with lid. 6.5" high. $250-300.

Left: Ceramic stein with attached lid, A & Eagle on front. 6" high. $750-1000.

Busch Gardens tea cup, Los Angeles, c. 1960. 3" high. $50-75.

Above: Set of five heavy embossed beer glasses, c. 1890. 6.75" high. $75-100 each.

Left: Detail from one the embossed glasses.

Top: Three small cylindrical beer glasses, c. 1900. Notice the earlier A & Eagle trademark on the glass in the center. 3.5" high. Left: $125-150; Center: $300-400; Right: $125-150.

Center: Pair of small Bevo glasses. 3.5" high. $35-50 each.

Left: Early Budweiser glass with A & Eagle design. 6.5" high. $300-350.

Set of Busch Extra Dry Ginger Ale glasses. 4.75" high. $50-75 each.

Michelob beer glasses in assorted sizes and
shapes. Back row, from left: $45-50; $15-25;
$75-100. Front row: $20-30 each.

Three additional Michelob beer glasses. Left: $25-35;
Center: $50-60; Right: $15-20.

Two of the Michelob glasses from the groupings opposite.

Budweiser and Michelob beer glasses. Heights range from 3" to 7". From left: $50-60; $15-20; $35-40; $20-30.

Two additional Michelob glasses.
Left: $35-40; Right: $50-60.

Budweiser glass. 5" high. $10-20.

Above: Assortment of Budweiser glasses, tall pilsner in the center. Heights range from 3" to 8". $10-20 each.

Left: Beer glass, St. Louis Beer, 1966. 5" high. $35-45.

Right & below: Barrel shaped Budweiser holiday glasses. 3" high. $10-20 each.

Another Budweiser holiday glass. 3" high. $25-35.

Anheuser-Busch beer glass, c. 1959. 7" high. $35-45.

Chapter 12

Commemoratives

"Budweiser's Greatest Triumph," c. 1903-1904, commemorates an award won by the Anheuser-Busch Brewing Association from the Bohemian Brewing Institute. Understandably proud of his recognition from Bohemia, once the world's leading brewing region, Adolphus Busch celebrated the occasion with this majestic print. $1500-2000.

Gold beer bottle, bottled from the 10,000,000th barrel, December 15, 1964. Bottle: 9.5" high. $100-150.

At 10:34 A.M. December 15, 1964 Anheuser-Busch produced its 10,000,000th barrel of the year.

Never before in history has any brewer in the world produced ten million barrels in one year. To Anheuser-Busch, of course, this industry record is a tremendous source of satisfaction.

More than that, it is a clear indication of the successful cooperation of American management and labor... of the continued growth of America's prosperity...of the ability of superior products to win ever-increasing acceptance in the marketplace.

As a memento of this occasion we would like you to have what we believe will be a collector's item...this special bottle of BUDWEISER®, which was bottled from the 10,000,000th barrel.

Above: Tin tray honoring the 100 Year Anniversary of Anheuser-Busch, 1876-1976, adorned with pictures of the brewery, the Clydesdales, Budweiser labels, and three of the company leaders. 13.5" x 19". $25-35.

Right: Plastic platter from 1977 sales convention, original St. Louis brewery in center surrounded by additional brewery locations. 21.5" x 15". $35-45.

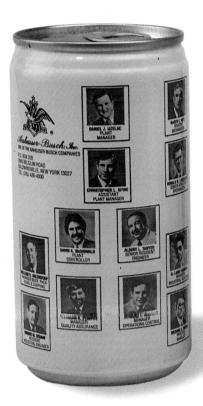 

Above: Commemorative Anheuser-Busch beer cans, c. 1980s. $15-25 each.

Left: Reverse of the commemorative beer cans.

Anheuser-Busch commemorative keychain also celebrating "10,000,000 Barrels, Dec. 15, 1964." Reverse is inscribed "Thanks" along with the signature of August A. Busch Jr. $35-40.

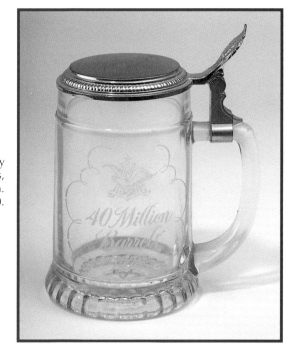

Glass stein, "Forty Million Barrels, 1978." 5.5" high. $50-60.

Above: Wooden desk plaque, "Fifty Million Barrels," 1980. 6" x 3". $75-100.

Right: Light up acrylic plaque on wooden base, "Sixty Million Barrels," 1983. $50-75.

Chapter 13

Corkscrews and Pocket Knives

As advertising became more diverse in the late nineteenth century, the concept of giveaway items grew in popularity. It's easy to understand why, as present-day companies still find that offering consumers some helpful little device is a handy way of gaining their loyalty. Better yet, adorning a giveaway with the company name or logo increases the likelihood that the consumer will remember to purchase the item again. As Ketchum notes, "[i]t didn't take long for advertisers to figure out that if an attractive design and catchy slogan would draw business, a useful gadget would do even better" (Ketchum 1977).

Corkscrews and pocket knives were among the most prevalent giveaways circulated by Anheuser-Busch. They had all the important criteria for success: they were small, inexpensive to produce, indispensable

for opening beer bottles (sealed at that time with a cork and wire bail), and easily decorated with the Anheuser-Busch name or logo. Many of the pocket knives carry the name of Adolphus Busch instead of the company name; in fact, Adolphus reportedly used such knives in place of calling cards when meeting with other businessmen. Certainly not one for humility, he added a unique feature to the knives: a peek through the small hole at one end reveals the countenance of none other than Adolphus Busch himself.

Above & left: Anheuser-Busch advertising corkscrews, c. 1890-1910. 5.5" average length. $20-35 each.

Above: Anheuser-Busch bar mounted corkscrew. 12" long. $750-1000.

Right: Detail of the bar mounted corkscrew, showing the A & Eagle logo.

Below: Set of small Anheuser-Busch corkscrews, c. 1950. 2.5" high. $50-75 each.

Above three: Adolphus Busch pocket knives, sometimes used by Adolphus as calling cards, c. 1890-1904. Note the small "peephole" on the end through which one could view a picture of Adolphus. Small: 2" long. Large: 3.25" long. $300-400 each with picture; $150-250 each without picture.

Right: Pocket knife showing brewery buildings, c. 1890-1904. 3.25" long. $300-400 with picture; $150-250 without picture.

Above: Set of three Anheuser-Busch pocket knives, two with mother-of-pearl insets, c. 1890-1904. 3.25" average length. $150-250 each.

Ornately decorated Anheuser-Busch pocket knives, c. 1890-1904. 3" average length. $300-400 each with picture; $150-250 each without picture.

Pocket knives and leather case, c. 1890-1904. 3" average length. Left: $75-100; Right: $150-200.

Chapter 14

Matchsafes, Matches, & Smoking Accessories

$150-200.

$150-200.

$250-300.

Above & following three pages: Matchsafes, small containers designed to hold wooden matches in one's pocket, were widely used as promotional items by Anheuser-Busch. This selection, most decorated with the A & Eagle logo, date from c. 1890-1904. Two of the matchsafes illustrate the locomotive and tender of a railroad car. Approximately 3" long each.

$200-250 each.

$175-200.

$150-200.

$150-200 each.

$200-250.

$150-200.

$150-200 each.

$300-350.

$150-200.

$150-200.

$150-200.

$300-350.

Cardboard matchbox, "Compliments of Adolphus Busch." 3" x .75". $100-150.

Two Budweiser matchbooks. $5-10 each.

These cardboard cans for holding stick matches advertise Busch Beer. This brand was first introduced in 1955. $5-10 each.

Small lighter shaped like a Budweiser beer bottle. $35-50.

Above: Anheuser-Busch brass ashtray, c. 1930. 4.75" x 6.5". $75-100.

Right: A more contemporary ashtray, asserting Budweiser beer as "deep in the heart of Texas." 5" dia. $10-15.

Chapter 15

Coasters

A selection of cardboard drink coasters, c. 1930, advertising Budweiser and Michelob brand beers.

$15-20.

$10-15 each.

$15-20 each.

$20-25 each.

$10-15.

$10-15 each.

$5-10 each.

Chapter 16

Jewelry, Keys, and Keychains

Elegant Anheuser-Busch cuff links and stick pin,
initials "AAB" on back of cuff links. $1000-1500.

Ruby and diamond charm and stick pin.
Charm: $2500 and up; Stick pin: $1500 and up.

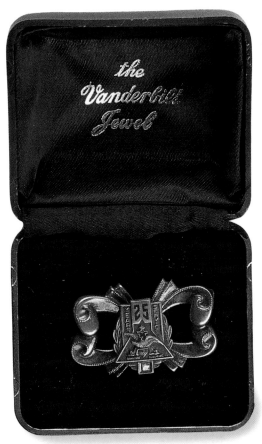

Employee pin for twenty-five years of service,
gold-plated with diamond, c. 1940. $100-200.

Budweiser "World Cup '86"
pin. 1" high. $25-30.

Two small A & Eagle pins. $100-125 each.

Anheuser-Busch cuff links, red and silver
with A & Eagle design. No price available.

Matching set of Anheuser-Busch cuff links and tie clasp. $35-50 for set.

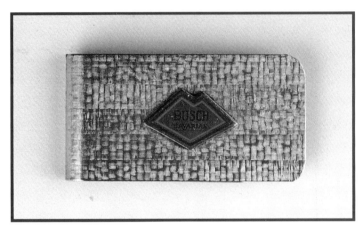

Money clip, "Busch Bavarian." 2" long. $10-15.

Money clip with gold A & Eagle. 2. 25" long. $35-40.

Belt buckle, A & Eagle encircled by foliage. 2.5" x 1.5". $40-50.

Left: Two Anheuser-Busch watch fobs, horseshoes with A & Eagle, c. 1918. 5" long. $150-175 each.

Above: Anheuser-Busch hat clip, used to hold hat on button or belt when not being worn. 3.5" long. $50-75.

Right: Anheuser-Busch key and keychain. 4.75" overall length. $25-30.

Pair of Anheuser-Busch keys. Reverse of the gold key reads "Availability Success." These and the other keys on this page were probably given by the company to local distributors. 2.75" long. $25-30 each.

"Busch Bavarian Beer" key with built-in thermometer. 5" long. $25-30.

Chapter 17

Miscellany

Metal advertising tripod for Malt-Nutrine,
c. 1890. 10.5" high. $350-500.

Bronze wall plaque, "Compliments of Adolphus Busch," c. 1891. 12" dia. $100-150.

Above: Anheuser-Busch playing cards. The green set has pictures of Anheuser-Busch products, the brown set features famous people on the face cards. $250-350 each.

Below: Another set of Anheuser-Busch playing cards. $75-100.

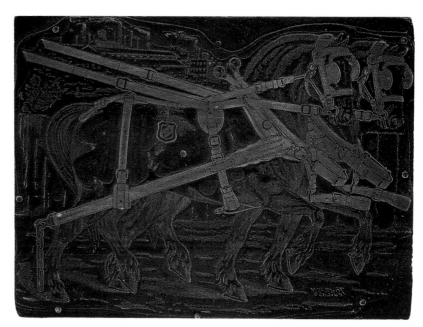

Clydesdale hitch printing plate,
c. 1905. 5" x 3.75". $75-100.

Etched glass shaker, A & Eagle.
5.5" high. $40-50.

Anheuser-Busch cane,
eagle handle. 34.5" long.
$500-750.

Two Anheuser-Busch cigar labels, c. 1900.
Top: $200-250. Bottom: $300-350.

Framed set of vintage bottle labels for Faust, Old Pale, Anheuser Lager, and Budweiser, c. 1900. $150-200.

Anheuser-Busch grain or flour sack. 21" x 37". $100-150.

Left: Beer foam scrapers, c. 1930. Made of plastic, metal, or other materials, scrapers like these were originally used to remove the foam from vessels of beer. They also provided another advertising mode for many breweries, which distributed them free to taverns that sold their beer. $40-60 each.

Below: Metal shelf markers, c. 1930. 14" long. $100-125 each.

Assorted bottle openers. The two at top are made of cast iron, c. 1910. The one on the right is a can opener as well; it reads "This calls for Bud" on one side and "Honorary Budweiser Brewmaster" on the reverse. $25-35 each.

Budweiser bottle caps, c. 1930s-1940s. $5-10 each.

Bank made from a Barley Malt Syrup can, c. 1930. 3" high. $100-125.

Tin can lid from Barley Malt Syrup, unused, c. 1930. 4.5" dia. $35-45.

Above: Metal advertising thermometer, c. 1935. Notice the assurance that Anheuser-Busch products came "as you like it, in bottles, in cans." 6" dia. $100-150.

Right: Electric light in the shape of a Barley Malt Syrup can. 8" high. $250-300.

Anheuser-Busch draught beer profit calculator, logos for Busch, Budweiser, and Michelob in the center. 6.5" dia. $20-30.

Detail of the dispenser's front.

Anheuser-Busch crock with same front design as the dispenser. 5" high. $300-350.

Crockery base dispenser used for Anheuser-Busch malt drink, c. 1910. 18" high. $250-300.

Novelty half bottle filled with malt, rice, hops, etc. Shown from the front, side, and back. 9.5" high. $50-75.

Light up tavern sign, Busch Bavarian Beer, c. 1960. 13" x 6.5". $35-50.

Light up Budweiser sign with horses grazing. 19" x 14". $75-100.

Medallion with attached ribbon, "Anheuser-Busch Ambassadors." 3" dia. No price available.

Small gold A & Eagle. 4.5" x 3.5". $35-50.

Anheuser-Busch souvenir Mardi Gras coins, 1968 and 1970. $10-15 each.

Another Mardi Gras coin. $10-15.

Pretzel holder for bar top use, c. 1930. 14" high. $125-150.

Left: Two advertising pocket mirrors for Buschtee and Kaffo, non-alcoholic beverages made briefly during Prohibition, c. 1920s. 2.75" wide. $150-175 each. Shown with celluloid covered pinback button, "I play on the Budweiser 1941 3,000,000 barrel team." 2.5" dia. $50-60.

Below: Left: pinback button with Clydesdale horse. $10-15. Right: advertising pocket mirror for Anheuser-Busch Ginger Ale. $75-100.

Malt-Nutrine string holder.
9" high. $1500-2000.

Assorted cutting utensils. From top: Budweiser knife, white plastic handle. 6.75" long. $35-40; letter opener, c. 1904. 8" long. $35-40; August Busch razor, one from a set of seven daily razors. 6" long. $200-250.

Budweiser salt and pepper shakers. Left: 4" high. $10-15. Above: 3.5" high. $10-15. Right: 2.5" high. $20-25.

Framed round sign,
"Anheuser-Busch on
Draught" A & Eagle in
center. 12" dia. $200-250.

Beer tap knobs, Budweiser and Michelob,
c. 1930-1940. $60-75 each.

Anheuser-Busch beer spigot,
c. 1910. The hook on the end
was to hold the handle of a
wire pail. 6" long. $60-90.

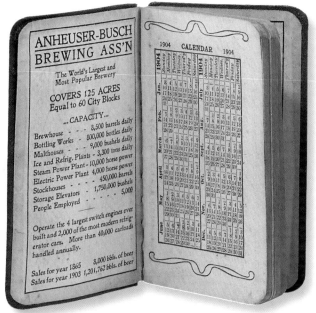

Salesman's note booklets, c. 1904. 2.5" x 4.25"
each. Left: $75-100; Center & right: $50-75.

Anheuser-Busch
Malt-Nutrine
album of transfer
pictures. 4" x 2.5".
$35-50.

Six pack of Anheuser-
Busch "Drinking
Water." $25-35.

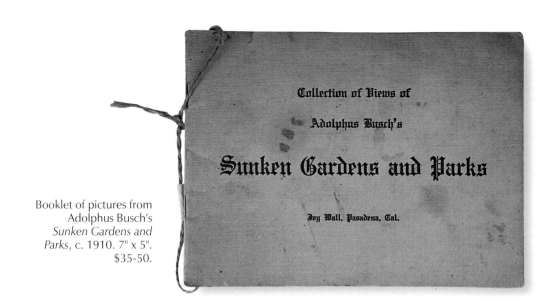

Collection of Views of

Adolphus Busch's

Sunken Gardens and Parks

Ivy Wall, Pasadena, Cal.

Booklet of pictures from Adolphus Busch's *Sunken Gardens and Parks*, c. 1910. 7" x 5". $35-50.

Residence of Adolphus Busch.

Snow on the Mountains, Seen from Sunken Gardens.

Inside pages from the *Sunken Gardens and Parks* booklet.

General View of Arroyo Garden.

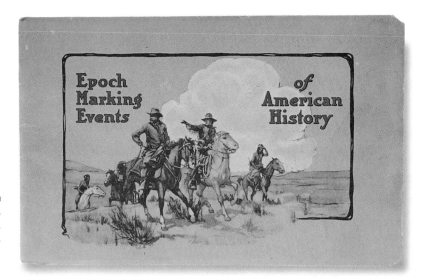

Anheuser-Busch advertising booklet, western theme, c. 1910. 9" x 5.75". $50-75.

Above: Stylized metal and wood advertising plaque, c. 1957. 13" x 10.5". $100-125.

Right: Half bottle, wood, "N. Giannini & Co., Wholesaler of the Month, Jan. 1966." 14" high. $50-75.

Plastic A & Eagle with round base, "Budweiser." 13" high, base 9.5" dia. $50-75.

Large wooden A & Eagle sculpture. 24" x 30". $200-350.

Bibliography

Anderson, Will. *The Beer Book: An Illustrated Guide to American Breweriana*. Princeton, New Jersey: The Pyne Press, 1973.

Anheuser-Busch Photo Album. St. Louis, Missouri: Anheuser-Busch, Inc., 1986.

Annual Report, 1997. St. Louis, Missouri: Corporate Communications Department, Anheuser-Busch Companies.

A Simple Story of the Origin and Unprecedented Growth of the Anheuser-Busch Brewing Association. St. Louis, Missouri: Anheuser-Busch Brewing Association, 1889 (Reprinted 1993).

Coleman, Alix, and Steven D. Price. *All the King's Horses: The Story of the Budweiser Clydesdales*. New York: The Viking Press, 1983.

Cope, Jim. *Old Advertising*. Burnet, Texas: Eakin Publications, 1980.

Fact Book, 1997/1998. St. Louis, Missouri: Corporate Communications Department, Anheuser-Busch Companies, Inc., 1997.

Haydock, Herbert A., and Helen I. Haydock. *The World of Beer Memorabilia: Identification and Value Guide*. Paducah, Kentucky: Collector Books, 1997.

Hughes, Stephen. *Pop Culture Mania: Collecting 20th-Century Americana for Fun and Profit*. New York: McGraw-Hill Book Company, 1984.

Ketchum Jr., William C. *Catalog of American Antiques*. New York: Rutledge Books, 1977.

——. *The Catalog of American Collectibles*. New York: Mayflower Books, Inc., 1979.

Krebs, Roland, in collaboration with Percy J. Orthwein. *Making Friends is Our Business: 100 Years of Anheuser-Busch*. Anheuser-Busch, Inc., The Cuneo Press, Inc., 1953.

Logan, Michael. "Reverse on Glass Advertising: Old Art Form Survives in California." *American Breweriana Journal* (September-October, 1997): 22-23.

Margolin, Victor, Ira Brichta, and Vivian Brichta. *The Promise and the Product: 200 Years of American Advertising Posters*. New York: Macmillan Publishing Co., Inc., 1979.

Sanders, W. Eugene, and Christine C. Sanders. *Pocket Matchsafes: Reflections of Life & Art, 1840-1920*. Atglen, Pennsylvania: Schiffer Publishing, Ltd., 1997.

Straub, Gary. *Collectible Beer Trays*. Atglen, Pennsylvania: Schiffer Publishing, Ltd., 1995.

The Beer Cans of Anheuser-Busch: An Illustrated History. St. Louis, Missouri: Anheuser-Busch, Inc., 1978.

The History of Anheuser-Busch Companies—A Fact Sheet. St. Louis, Missouri: Anheuser-Busch Companies, Inc., 1995.

Index